W9-AHX-768

DISCOVER THE SECRETS OF THE EVIDENCE WITH . . .

SCIENTISTS in ACTION!

Crime Scene Techs!

7

MC

SCIENTISTS in ACTION!

Archaeologists!

Climatologists!

Astronauts!

Crime Scene Techs!

Big-Animal Vets!

Cyber Spy Hunters!

Biomedical Engineers!

Marine Biologists!

Civil Engineers!

Robot Builders!

Crime Scene Techs!

By Beth Sutinis

Mason Crest
450 Parkway Drive, Suite D
Broomall, PA 19008
www.masoncrest.com

Printed and bound in the United States of America.

Series ISBN: 978-1-4222-3416-7
Hardback ISBN: 978-1-4222-3423-5
EBook ISBN: 978-1-4222-8484-1

First printing
1 3 5 7 9 8 6 4 2

Produced by Shoreline Publishing Group LLC
Santa Barbara, California
Editorial Director: James Buckley Jr.
Designer: Tom Carling, Carling Design Inc.
Production: Sandy Gordon
www.shorelinepublishing.com
Cover image: Dreamstime.com/CorepicsVof

Library of Congress Cataloging-in-Publication Data is on file with the publisher.

Contents

Key Icons to Look For

Words to Understand: These words with their easy-to-understand definitions will increase the reader's understanding of the text, while building vocabulary skills.

Sidebars: This boxed material within the main text allows readers to build knowledge, gain insights, explore possibilities, and broaden their perspectives by weaving together additional information to provide realistic and holistic perspectives.

Research Projects: Readers are pointed toward areas of further inquiry connected to each chapter. Suggestions are provided for projects that encourage deeper research and analysis.

Text-Dependent Questions: These questions send the reader back to the text for more careful attention to the evidence presented here.

Series Glossary of Key Terms: This back-of-the-book glossary contains terminology used throughout this series. Words found here increase the reader's ability to read and comprehend higher-level books and articles in this field.

Action!

akayla Isaacs walked up to the apartment building. She wasn't going home, she was going to work. Makayla was a **DNA** specialist who worked at the county medical examiner's office. The police department in her small city wasn't large enough to have specialists in its crime scene unit. For more complex crimes that required DNA collection, they phoned specialists from the M.E.'s office—and Makayla was called into action!

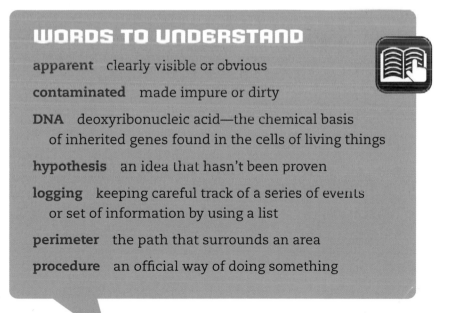

WORDS TO UNDERSTAND

apparent   clearly visible or obvious

contaminated   made impure or dirty

DNA   deoxyribonucleic acid—the chemical basis of inherited genes found in the cells of living things

hypothesis   an idea that hasn't been proven

logging   keeping careful track of a series of events or set of information by using a list

perimeter   the path that surrounds an area

procedure   an official way of doing something

Crime scene investigators, police officers, and detectives all must carefully follow proper procedure when searching for clues.

Over the phone, Detective Robert Farley had briefed Makayla about a string of robberies that had plagued the city. Farley reported that officers responding to a 911 call had arrived to find the apartment's resident injured at the scene of an **apparent** robbery. The officers got the victim medical help, then they properly secured the scene by setting up a **perimeter**, and called in the detectives. When Farley arrived, he checked in with the officer who had secured the perimeter. It was her job to write down the names of all the people who came and went from the crime scene. She was also in charge of keeping out anyone who did not absolutely need to be there. There's a reason they call it "police **procedure**," since following procedure precisely is crucial to keeping the evidence from being **contaminated**, which might make it useless in court.

At the scene, two crime scene investigators (CSIs) went in first, taking video, photographs, and notes. They walked in a spiral pattern starting from the middle of the room, where the victim had awoken with a gash on his head. The investigators documented everything in the scene. The CSIs reported what they saw to the evidence collection team—an open file cabinet and a baseball bat, apparently with blood on it. Farley also observed a few things that made him think the robbery might be connected to other crimes he was investigating. This time, however, the robbery had included an attack of the victim.

Detective Farley spoke to the victim, Mr. Ramos. Farley learned that the baseball bat belonged to Ramos. Farley did the interview, not the CSIs. It was important that the CSIs never speak to witnesses or suspects— more of that procedural stuff! The pros analyzing the evidence didn't want to be influenced by the impressions of others.

Detective Farley decided then to call Makayla. If this scene was anything like the others, there weren't going to be any fingerprints or shoe impressions or hairs to collect, although the CSIs would still look for such evidence. Farley was hoping there might be "touch" DNA on the baseball bat.

One of the tricky things about touch DNA was that so few cells were required for the process that everybody who walked into the scene could potentially leave their own body traces, even if they were wearing their PPE (personal protection equipment) correctly. It was best if DNA and touch DNA evidence were collected and secured first. So before the CSIs touched anything, Makayla suited up in her PPE outside the perimeter. She grabbed her kit and went right to the baseball bat, which was lying on the floor. It had been photographed and videotaped from every angle, but was untouched.

Touch DNA was most likely to be found where someone had touched something with pressure. Makayla used her gear to gather possible evidence from the bat's handle and also further up the grip. She then carefully bagged the baseball bat to take it back to the lab, where other workers would examine the blood on the bat's fat end. The blood was probably from the victim, so a sample from the victim would need to be obtained and analyzed to make a match.

Makayla took the bagged bat to the crime scene perimeter and handed it over to the CSI technician who was **logging** in evidence. As she walked out the door, Makayla spied something she didn't see when walking into the apartment.

"The baseball bat was a good place to start, but that is what I need to test," she said to Detective Farley who was standing on the other side of the tape. From his side of the perimeter tape, the detective could see that Makayla was pointing to something on the door of the apartment directly across from the crime scene. Before she reopened her kit, Makayla took a close look at the area where the peephole was on the neighbor's door. A peephole allows someone inside an apartment to look into the hall before opening the door. The peephole of the victim's neighbor was covered with something. There was a Band-Aid stuck to the outside of it!

A blood-stained knife goes directly into a sealed plastic bag for analysis. It may one day end up as evidence in a courtroom.

Makayla stood back and asked the forensic photographer to suit up again in a new PPE and come back into the crime scene. While she waited patiently for the photographer, she determined the best approach to collecting this particular evidence. By the time the pictures had been taken, she knew what to do.

She decided to scrape the edges and outside of the bandage into a collection envelope. Then, using tweezers, she gently removed the bandage and sealed it inside a second paper envelope. She labeled both envelopes and delivered them to the CSI. Then she examined the door itself in case any skin cells had been transferred there.

The DNA specialist noticed a Band-Aid covering a peephole such as this one. It was the breakthough police needed to make an arrest.

In the squad car on the way back to the lab, Makayla came up with a **hypothesis** that the robber had put the bandage over the peephole to prevent a neighbor from watching him come and go. The lack of care taken by an otherwise careful criminal may have been because the robber was used to ripping off the bandage as he left and taking it with him—leaving no visible trace it ever had been there. This time, in his haste, it looked like he forgot to do that.

Detective Farley could now go back to the other crime scenes with a trace evidence specialist who worked in the lab with Makayla. Although the bandages wouldn't be over the peepholes at other crime scenes, they might find traces of the adhesive itself on the doors, which would suggest a pattern. Band-Aid adhesive wasn't a common thing to find on peepholes, after all.

Weeks later, Makayla's theory proved correct. The adhesive turned up at other crime scenes, and a tiny piece of DNA was found on one door. Later, when a suspect was arrested, the DNA matched.

Science—and good detective work—came through to solve the crime.

The Scientists and Their Science

Scientists who work in the **forensic** sciences go where the action is. They visit crime scenes wherever they occur—in busy cities, in empty fields, in tunnels, in office buildings, anywhere. Forensic science is all about variety. Not only do the scientists find evidence in hundreds of places, but there are dozens of different **disciplines** within forensic science. Each of them seeks to figure out what really happened.

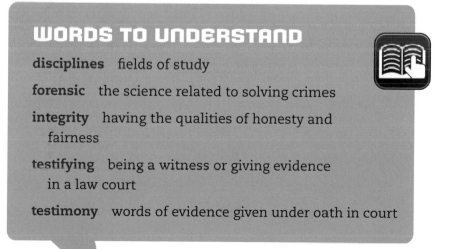

WORDS TO UNDERSTAND

disciplines   fields of study

forensic   the science related to solving crimes

integrity   having the qualities of honesty and fairness

testifying   being a witness or giving evidence in a law court

testimony   words of evidence given under oath in court

Counterfeit money is fake money that is a near-exact copy of the real thing. A forensic scientist can spot the differences that an untrained eye cannot.

Forensic science uses the scientific method to gather and examine information about the past whenever there is a question of law. The legal system deals with civil issues, such as "Did rich Uncle George really sign that will?" To make sure, you would need a handwriting analyst and a trace evidence specialist. Legal matters include criminal issues, such as "Who stole Farmer Brown's lettuce?" To figure that one out, you might call in a bite-mark analyst. Even financial crimes can be solved with forensic science. Did a company hide money from the government? Call in a forensic accountant to find out!

Forensic science goes all the way back to ancient history. The Greek scientist Archimedes may have helped resolve a dispute between the Greek king Hiero and a goldsmith. The goldsmith may have tried to cheat the king out of the proper amount of gold in a crown. Archimedes used a test to show that the goldsmith had tried to pass some of the gold off as silver! He used a test that is not very different from the one used today. A thousand years later, in China, the first book of forensics was published. It included information about how to tell the difference between a drowning and death by strangulation. Since there has been law, forensic experts have used scientific means to solve disputes.

In more recent times, advancements in technology have allowed forensic science to play a bigger and more important role in solving crimes. Eyewitness **testimony**—once the most important evidence presented in criminal cases—has come under fire as scientists show that human memory is not always perfect. Forensic science evidence is filling this void.

Where's the Action?

*T*here are at least 30 different areas of study in forensic science. Here are some of the hottest topics:

DNA: Isolating copies of unique molecules located in cells to determine the source of body materials from humans, animals, or plants (see page 18 for more on DNA).

Mitochondrial DNA (mtDNA): A type of evidence recovered from old, damaged, or very small samples of human body material. Even with tiny amounts, scientists can learn a great deal.

DNA

Deoxyribonucleic acid, or DNA, is a chemical found in nearly every cell in people, animals, and plants. DNA is a code or recipe for growing new life. DNA is unique to individuals, so no two people have exactly the same DNA. People in the same family can have similar DNA markers—those are variations found on specific places on the molecule. DNA markers are responsible for certain traits in people, such as brown eyes or curly hair.

The DNA molecule can be viewed under a powerful microscope in a laboratory. It looks like a ladder coiled and twisted around. This structure is known as a double helix.

DNA analysts isolate and view those shapes, then compare them to other samples. If a match is made, DNA can prove that a person was present at a crime scene or was responsible for a crime.

DNA can be collected from a person's cheek.

Crime scene reconstruction: Using information from blood-pattern analysis, the flight path of projectiles such as bullets or blood, trace evidence, and many other areas to re-create crime scenes for study.

Criminalistics: The recognition, identification, analysis, and assessment of physical evidence. Criminalists have a broad knowledge covering most of the different disciplines of forensic science.

Digital forensic science: Recovering and investigating information found on digital devices such as computers.

Fingerprint analysis: The analysis of the unique pattern left behind by the oils on fingers when a solid surface is touched. This is one of the oldest forensic sciences.

Hair and fiber analysis: Reviewing hairs and fibers to determine their source.

Tire-tread impressions: The unique pattern evidence left by vehicles in soil, pavement, or other surfaces.

Toxicology: Investigating drug use or poisoning.

Touch DNA: Tiny numbers of cells left behind by people where no visible stain is present.

Everyone's fingerprints—such as these left behind and collected for evidence—are unique. Fingerprint analysis is one of the oldest forensic sciences.

All the pieces of the crime scene puzzle are photographed, noted, and documented before the site is disturbed in any way.

The Science of Crime

*I*t's all about procedure—following processes that are known to work well to reach accurate conclusions. Many job descriptions stress wanting candidates who are "detail oriented." In crime scene work, it's all in the details. Following the scientific method—asking and answering questions by making observations and doing experiments—is critical in forensic science. That's not just because being accurate is important; it's because the science of crime scene work must be reported in courts, so it can be understood by members of a jury, who may have no science training.

When approaching a crime scene, investigators first need to decide what's important. The crime scene is properly controlled, then observations are made. Using their senses, crime scene investigators look, listen, and smell the surroundings. That kind of action does not call for touching—yet! The evidence shouldn't be disturbed before it's collected. Next, making a hypothesis will direct the evidence collection. A hypothesis is an idea you can test. Ask a question such as, "What happened here?" The possible answers will guide the action.

Then, collect data. In the case of forensic science, the data is the evidence that is gathered. Don't forget to document that data! Photos and video are great, but taking detailed notes at every stage of work is critical. Once the evidence is collected and securely brought to the lab, the tests happen. Technology is how science gets done.

The test results may be in, but the job isn't done. The results must be analyzed; experts give their opinion of what the facts show. Being able to document those findings in clear and concise reports is crucial. That's the action of forensic science, after all—applying the facts to the law. That leads to presenting the findings in written statements to police and officers of the court, and sometimes by **testifying** in court.

Becoming a Crime Scene Technician

CSI should attend college and study forensic science or another science such as biology or chemistry, plus take courses in math and composition. Working hard and earning good grades is important, since further education is necessary and training programs after college are hard to get into.

If students are very sure about their career path by the time they leave high school, there are specialized programs for undergraduates. Some colleges that feature such programs include John Jay College of

Why I Became a Criminalist

"I have loved science and puzzles since I was a child," said Ralph Ristenbatt. "I always knew I would become a scientist; my interests spanned many sciences, including astronomy, oceanography, meteorology, and chemistry." Ristenbatt earned a degree in biochemistry, but wanted to find a career with more diversity. He completed graduate school with a master of science degree in forensic science and accepted a job with the Office of Chief Medical Examiner in New York City. "My job," he said, "was exactly what I had always wanted: a combination of laboratory and field work. Experienced criminalists are equally capable in the laboratory and at crime scenes."

After 16 years in New York City, Ristenbatt became a teacher in the forensic science program at Pennsylvania State University. He instructs undergraduate and graduate students in crime scene investigation.

Criminal Justice in New York City, Penn State University, and the University of California at Davis. Even for students who aren't as sure what they want to study in college, postgraduate degrees and continuing education courses are available as pathways to forensic science careers.

Training is the next step. Students often pursue internships during undergraduate education. Internships and fellowships—postgrad jobs—at places such as the Central Intelligence Agency (CIA), Federal Bureau of Investigation (FBI), Department of Justice (DOJ), and regional crime laboratories offer hands-on experience to young criminalists.

The American Board of Criminalistics gives tough exams to pros already working in the field. If they pass, the certificates they earn can help them get better jobs or more responsibility.

Learning from others with on-the-job training is where most CSIs really perfect their craft. A small-town sheriff's office may be doing almost all of its own forensic science work unless a major crime is committed. A big-city morgue may seem like a more glamorous location for crime, but the work there for lower-level employees may be repetitive. Unlike in a small town, it could take many years to acquire a wide range of skills working in a big department.

CSIs need to be curious, precise in their work habits, and have **integrity**. Even a legal case that isn't about a murder matters to someone or to the community at large. Telling the truth even if it isn't convenient or will keep a bad guy out of jail is crucial. Plus, all career paths in forensic sciences involve extensive background checks—so the integrity that counts is both personal and professional.

 Text-Dependent Questions

1. Is crime scene investigation a new science?

2. Is it possible to become a forensic scientist if one doesn't study it in college?

3. Name one government agency that offers internships in crime scene investigation.

Research Project

Write a cover letter for a job as a crime scene tech. What qualities do you have that would make you a good one? What area of forensic science would you want to specialize in? Consider the different specialties to decide.

WORDS TO UNDERSTAND

acquittal   a not guilty verdict in court

autoclave   a chamber that sterilizes equipment at high heat and pressure

ballistics   the science of things that can be launched, such as bullets, bombs, and rockets

bindles   special paper that can be folded to make small envelopes

biohazard   organisms that pose a threat to living things

biometrics   technology that measures human body characteristics

electrostatic   electric charges that don't move

mass spectrometers   lab machines that can determine what chemicals make up a sample

sterilized   to make free from bacteria or other living organisms

Tools of the Trade

Scientists need gear to succeed. Forensic science laboratory work calls for computers, measuring instruments, microscopes, cutting tools, and cool specialized machines such as **mass spectrometers**.

Fieldwork gear needs to be portable; some big cities have vans that act like mobile labs and go straight to the crime scene, but in smaller towns, forensic scientists have to carry everything they need. That includes handheld kits that hold swabs, envelopes, **bindles**, evidence bags, tweezers, cutting instruments, flashlights, and much more.

PPE

*P*ersonal protective equipment—or PPE—is the term for the disposable suit that CSIs wear at a crime scene. A PPE consists of coveralls often made of the space-age fabric Tyvek. CSIs also wear a hair covering, mask, protective eyewear, booties, and gloves. In most situations in which workers wear PPE, they do so to protect themselves from elements in the work environment. A person working around dangerous chemicals might wear PPE to keep the chemicals out. In crime scene work, the PPE does the opposite. The clothing protects the evidence from the worker! Contaminating a crime scene is as easy as sneezing without a mask on or tracking cat hair into a scene from the outside. The PPE contains anything personal—the smallest fiber or a tiny bead of sweat could make the difference between an **acquittal** and a conviction in court.

Crime Scene Kit

*C*leaned and **sterilized** or disposable: Nearly everything in a crime scene kit has to be free of even microscopic trace elements. If not, then the items are single-use and are thrown out either as industrial waste or **biohazard** material. Again, avoiding contamination is the name of the game.

Tools in the kit are super-specialized. Cutting tools are a good example. A CSI's kit might have multiple types of scissors, scalpels, and box cutters. Each is good for cutting different types of materials in a variety of situations with precision.

In cities and at regional crime labs, the team will be larger and more specialized, so individuals carry kits that help with a particular

Whether collecting fingerprints, blood, or other evidence, everything an investigator needs is in the crime scene kit.

job, such as collecting fingerprints, body fluids, or blood, or making castings from impressions.

In smaller locales where a crime scene unit might be one person or a small team of police officers, a kit will have all the general needs for crime scene investigation: evidence collection equipment, a notebook, camera, photographic scale (ruler), sketch paper, pencils and

An electrostatic dust print lifter enables crime scene investigators to pick up clues even the most careful criminals are sure to leave behind.

pens, plus the more specialized kits. It's a lot of gear to keep track of and to keep clean and in good working order, but CSIs accept this as part of the job.

Digging for Dust

One of the coolest bits of crime scene equipment is the **electrostatic** dust print lifter. When someone walks through an area, dust, fine dirt, and other particles of matter can be transferred from their shoes to the surfaces they walked. These impressions can be preserved and transferred back to the lab for analysis. In the past, photographs would have to do.

The electrostatic machine works by charging a plastic film with static energy. The film is placed over the dusty impression, which lifts onto the plastic (just like when you pull off a piece of plastic from its roll and it sticks to your hands before you can wrap your dish with it). The impression is then analyzed just as a footprint made in mud and cast in plaster would be.

Where They Work

Crime can occur anywhere, so crime scene investigators can end up working in unusual places. Fieldwork is just one type of workplace for CSIs. After the evidence is collected, it travels securely to a crime lab, which can be at a medical examiner's office, a regional laboratory center, or a major government institution. One of those government sites is the FBI Laboratory Division at the Marine Corps Base in Quantico, Virginia.

Founded in 1932, the FBI laboratory is actually a massive campus of buildings. More than 500 scientists work in disciplines ranging from **biometric** analysis (DNA, fingerprints) to cryptanalysis (code-breaking) to explosives, and dozens of other areas of study.

At a city or county lab, care will have been taken to plan the work space. Flexibility in that space is important because science is changing, just like crime. A lab built 25 years ago might not have any space devoted to DNA analysis, since that was a new area then. Making sure the space is not too cramped or cluttered is important both for avoiding contamination and for workplace safety. Dangerous chemicals and tools are all over a crime lab, which is why an emergency shower, eyewash stations, and sinks are important features.

Benches for spreading out work and conducting experiments are key, too, as is having lots of secure storage. Remember all that equipment? It has to be kept somewhere. An ideal lab will have about 800 square feet of work space for each scientist. That's the size of a small two-bedroom apartment!

Computers, refrigerator and freezer storage, and dozens of pieces of specialized lab equipment, such as an **autoclave**, X-ray machine, **ballistics** testing chamber, scanning electron microscope, and so much

Crime scene investigators use powerful microscopes in their labs. Even the tiniest bit of evidence might be enough to catch the bad guys!

more are found at the lab, as well as administrative offices, conference rooms, and a break room and locker room.

All the gear that CSIs use is aimed at finding the tiniest bits of evidence that will help police solve crimes…and the government put criminals away.

 **Text-Dependent Questions**

1. PPE is only important for protecting a crime scene tech from getting hurt on the job. Yes or no?

2. Why are crime labs designed to be open and easy to get around?

3. Can people in a family have the same DNA?

 **Research Project**

Do you like to cook? Even if you just like to eat, watching people cook can be really interesting. A crime scene lab has a lot in common with a kitchen—specialized equipment, the importance of following instructions, and desiring a good result. Choose a recipe to follow (or make up your own!). Write down the precise steps you follow in your own words, describing the equipment you use and how you use it. Start out by stating what you think the end result of the recipe will look, smell, and taste like. This is your hypothesis. At the end, be sure to say if your hypothesis was correct!

Tales From the Field!

Art Heist!

On March 18, 1990, two men dressed as police officers talked their way into the Isabella Stewart Gardner Museum in Boston, Massachusetts. After tying up the guards, the thieves made off with more than $500 million worth of paintings by great masters, including Rembrandt van Rijn and Johan Vermeer.

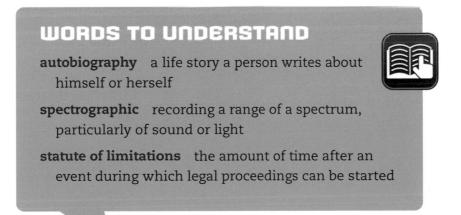

WORDS TO UNDERSTAND

autobiography   a life story a person writes about himself or herself

spectrographic   recording a range of a spectrum, particularly of sound or light

statute of limitations   the amount of time after an event during which legal proceedings can be started

This 1633 painting by Rembrandt (*The Storm on the Sea of Galilee*) was one of the treasures stolen.

The thieves got away, and the art has not been recovered despite thorough investigation by the local authorities and a special FBI team. In fact, over the years, the team has enlisted the help of the public many times.

In 2010, investigators realized that evidence collected and secured at the crime scene 20 years earlier might finally pay off. The duct tape that had been used to tie up the guards had been collected and stored. Now, with DNA technology, that tape might hold clues to the identities of the thieves. The **statute of limitations** on the actual robbery had long elapsed, but the thieves were the only known link to the missing precious art. Finding them was an important step toward getting the art home.

Recently, the identities of the thieves were discovered. Two of them are dead, and the third denies knowledge of the art's whereabouts. In the near future, it may be returned to the beautiful home of Mrs. Gardner. A long, careful investigation will have brought it there.

Hermit Billionaire?

Two authors thought up a scheme. They would write a fake **autobiography** of a famous man—Howard Hughes—who hadn't been seen in public in decades and sell it for big money to the highest bidder. The authors banked on Hughes refusing to come out of hiding even to defend himself against his fake life story.

Well, they were partly right. Hughes did not *come out* in public to make a statement against the authors. However, after contacting reporters to deny the book was legitimate, Hughes was willing to *speak* to reporters on the phone. During a conversation, his voice was recorded and put through **spectrographic** voiceprint analysis. The science confirmed it was Hughes's voice, when compared to voice samples from years earlier. The two authors were convicted and sent to jail. Some might say it turned out okay for at least one of them later. In 2008, a movie about the incident, *The Hoax*, hit theaters; it was based on a book with the same title by one of the "creative" authors.

Howard Hughes didn't come out of hiding after his "autobiography," but voiceprint analysis helped expose the hoax.

When You Gotta Go...

An important idea in forensic science is that "every contact leaves a trace." This means that criminals, especially in the intense circumstances of many crimes, likely will leave some trace of themselves at the scene of the crime—it might be as little as a hair, some saliva or blood, or dirt from their shoes. Other times, they will take something away with them from the crime scene, such as a trace of the victim's blood, dust on a jacket sleeve, or gunpowder residue on their hands.

In the case of a burglary in Oklahoma City, the robber left a lot more than a simple hair. After having relieved a victim of more than $1,000 in gaming equipment and clothing, burglar Charles Williams apparently couldn't hold it and used the victim's toilet—leaving what you might expect in the bowl, as well as used toilet tissue on the floor. The disgusting evidence was collected by police officers, processed, and matched to the suspect, which led to his arrest.

Brandt Cassidy, the laboratory director where the DNA evidence from the toilet was processed, said, "The type of analysis that's used today is very, very powerful. The skin cells that would have rubbed off when someone used that toilet paper would be sufficient to identify the person who left the sample there. You're shedding skin cells all the time, so you're leaving traces of your DNA everywhere you go. You can take any cell that had been living in that person and isolate DNA from it and develop a unique fingerprint from it that would represent that person."

Being a crime scene tech sometimes means having to deal with some rather unpleasant stuff . . . but that's part of the job!

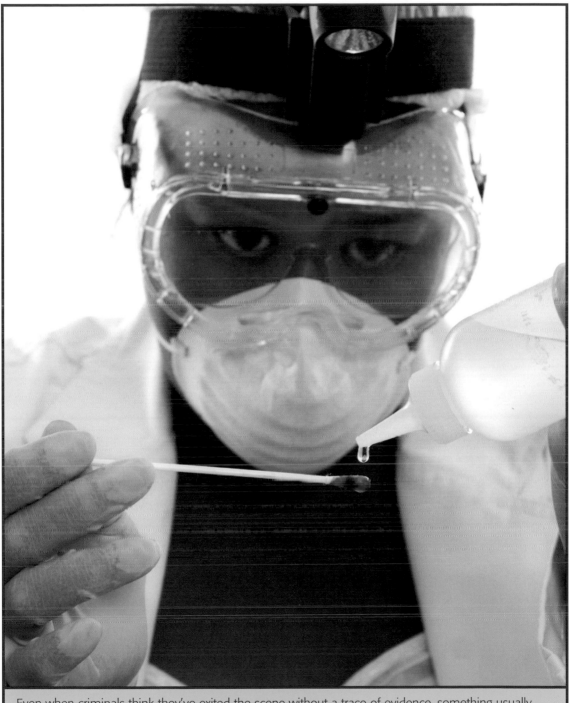

Even when criminals think they've exited the scene without a trace of evidence, something usually is left behind that allows investigators to find traces of DNA.

Has a convicted murderer been jailed for a crime he did not commit? New crime scene technology has some investigators rethinking a 1999 case.

Listening in to Crime

*T*rue crime stories have always gripped the public, but usually the news, a book, or a movie is the source material. One such story was broadcast to listeners via a podcast—in fact, it became the most listened-to podcast in history.

Serial, produced by a public radio team of journalists, is based on the 1999 murder of a high school student in Baltimore, Maryland. Another teen, Adnan Syed, was eventually convicted of the murder and is still in jail. Some people believe Syed to be innocent of the crime, or at least to have received an unfair trial. New lawyers are working on his behalf to see if he can get out of jail early.

Serial's listeners are divided on the question of Syed's guilt. However, they are not divided on the question of DNA evidence that was collected but never tested and analyzed. It was frustrating to them that a rope and clothing found near the victim's body was collected, determined to have biological material on it, but never tested.

One answer to why it wasn't tested is that in 1999, DNA testing was still new technology, and very expensive. Local law enforcement agencies pay for every test, and they have to answer for that decision. Also, back then, larger samples were needed to get results. Sometimes, if CSIs determined a sample wasn't large enough, they would hold evidence until a future date when the technology had improved. Lastly, and perhaps most importantly for the case in *Serial*, when there is solid evidence—in this case a witness willing to testify—authorities determined that additional proof wasn't required to prove guilt in court.

It remains to be seen if Adnan Syed, who has given permission for the DNA evidence in his case to be tested and analyzed, will leave jail early. What we also don't know is if the DNA evidence—now 16 years old—will show any results at all. Even in newer cases, DNA results are often inconclusive, meaning they may tell something about the source of the samples collected but not enough to tie one person to a crime. In any event, *Serial* fans hold their breath and await answers. Crime scene science is at the center of the tale. People listening have seen the popularity of fictional CSI TV shows. This is a case in which real life might be more dramatic than fiction.

Glass Tells Tales

A thief breaks a window to enter a high-end jewelry store, a mirror is broken in a struggle, a bullet penetrates a car's windshield…where crimes occur there is often glass. How do crime scene investigators and analysts in the lab get glass to give up its stories? The first step is careful evidence collection by the CSIs. Samples collected and preserved with minimal loss have the best chance of obtaining results. Glass is fragile when broken, of course. The chips and shards that come away from the glass can be as small as bits of dust or even powder.

"Glass is frequently recovered from crime scenes," explained Shirly Berends-Montero of the Netherlands Forensic Institute, "and because of its nature, it is easily transferred to anyone who has had direct or indirect contact with the crime scene. Improved techniques for glass analysis mean more reliable results for use in a court of law."

Those improved techniques include hitting glass samples with lasers in a mass spectrometer. The results can match samples to a single source. So if that thief who broke the jewelry store window ends up with tiny bits of glass on her jacket, CSIs can detect it and match it to the window with help from their colleagues in the lab.

The Truth, the Whole Truth...

*I*t would be easy to solve crimes if all investigators had to do was hook up a suspected criminal to a polygraph—more commonly called a "lie detector"—ask a few questions, and determine if he or she was telling the truth or not. Of course, it isn't that easy.

Forensics experts have used polygraph tests for nearly 100 years. The modern polygraph was invented by John A. Larson, a doctorate student at the University of California, in 1920. That same year, Larson joined the Berkeley Police Department. A polygraph machine already existed at the time, but Larson improved upon it by combining

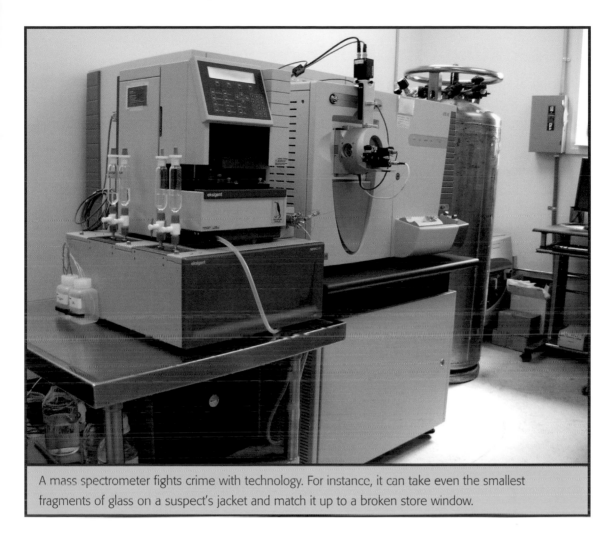

A mass spectrometer fights crime with technology. For instance, it can take even the smallest fragments of glass on a suspect's jacket and match it up to a broken store window.

blood-pressure figures with other readings such as pulse and respiration. He used his invention in his department's forensics investigations. He soon made headlines when his machine "proved" that a man suspected of killing a priest in San Francisco was lying about his involvment in the murder.

There's just one hitch, however: Polygraph results generally aren't admissable in today's United States court system. Opinions vary, but the machines are believed to be reasonably accurate—but not perfect.

Searching for Chemicals

Much of the equipment in a crime lab is specialized to the point where it only does one thing. The mass spectrometer, however, is kind of the opposite of that. It has so many applications that pretty much any substance can be broken down into one of the smallest chemical elements.

The machine analyzes the amount and type of chemicals in a sample. It can be adapted for toxicology (Is that white powder an illegal drug?), stomach contents (Was that person poisoned?), or arson investigation (Was gas used to start that fire?). Those are just a few examples.

How does the mass spectrometer do that? The sample being tested is hit with ions inside a machine with a curved chamber; the ions are sped up to super-speed, then their path is bent by strong magnets along the curve. The different ions bend into separate paths depending on how heavy they are. The streams are then analyzed electrically. The analysis identifies what the different elements are.

If the kinds of crime lab equipment were athletes, the mass spectrometer would be a five-tool baseball player: It can do it all!

Plus, it's been shown that proper coaching sometimes can help suspects fool the lie detector.

Still, talented scientists and law enforcement officials will continue to find ways to seek the truth. Crime scene investigation and forensic science use teamwork to apply science to real life. These are growing areas of study in which methodical pursuit of evidence seeks justice for crime victims. Anyone interested in just about any discipline of science can find a place in crime scene work, be it in the laboratory or in the field, at a crime scene near you.

Text-Dependent Questions

1. Why wasn't the evidence in the art heist at the museum tested for DNA in 1990?

2. Name a type of trace evidence someone might leave at a crime scene.

3. Why is glass easily transferred at a crime scene?

Research Project

Crime scene techs and forensic scientists use teamwork and precision to reach their goals. Can you think of a way you could use those traits to do a project that would benefit your community? Think of a project—maybe collecting food for a homeless shelter or staging a cleanup day at your local park. Next, make a step-by-step list of how you can get your project going. Look at the steps described in the text as they apply to crime scene and forensic science work. What do the two have in common? Grab some friends and follow through with your community project. Good luck!

Scientists in the News

Forensics Pioneer: One of the first forensic scientists in the news was ancient Rome's Marcus Fabius Quintilianus, more commonly known as Quintilian. In fact, when the attorney won an acquittal for his client in the first century BCE, he did it with one of the earliest known uses of forensics. Quintilian's client was a blind man who was accused of murdering his mother. The attorney proved that a bloody palm print found at the scene of the crime did not match the palm print of the accused man, who then was freed.

"The Father of DNA Evidence": Alec Jeffreys is a professor of genetics at the University of Leicester, where he has worked since 1977, in the United Kingdom. When Jeffreys began studying DNA in the late 1970s and early 1980s, scientists knew that families shared certain DNA characteristics. In 1984, however, Jeffreys discovered "DNA fingerprinting"—that is, that everyone's DNA is unique, just like a fingerprint is unique. For several years after his discovery, Jeffreys' lab was the only one in the world that did DNA fingerprinting; often it was used to determine paternity. Jeffreys quickly realized its application to criminal cases, and DNA fingerprinting is now commonly used in forensic police work. In 1994, Jeffreys was knighted for his contributions, and he is officially known as Professor Sir Alec Jeffreys.

Dr. G: In a high-profile case in 2008, Dr. Jan Garavaglia, the chief medical examiner in Orange and Osceola counties in Orlando, Florida, determined that two-year-old Caylee Anthony had been murdered. Three years later, Caylee's mother, who was accused of the killing, was

Dr. Jan Garavaglia, a top forensic scientist.

found not guilty after a lengthy trial. The verdict was roundly criticized on television and in social media. Many armchair "experts" felt that Garavaglia should have come to a more definitive conclusion about the exact cause of death and the murderer, just like they do at the end of popular television programs about crime scene investigations. Garavaglia cautioned, however, that real-life forensics is not TV. "My job is not to determine who did it," she told NBC's *The Today Show.* "My job is to determine what happened."

Even before the famous case, Garavaglia was one of the most recognizable forensics experts in the United States. In the late 1980s, one of Dr. G's first cases uncovered a scandal at a funeral home in Florida. In 2008, she penned a popular book called *How Not to Die: Surprising Lessons on Living Longer, Safer, and Healthier from America's Favorite Medical Examiner.*

From 2004 to 2012, Garavaglia hosted a reality television show on the Discovery Health Channel called *Dr. G: Medical Examiner.* She also has appeared on many national television shows (such as *The Oprah Winfrey Show, Larry King Live,* and *The Doctors*) as a forensics expert.

Find Out More

Books

Cooper, Chris. *Eyewitness Books: Forensic Science*. New York: DK Publishing, 2008.

James, Stuart H. and Jon J. Nordby. *Forensic Science: An Introduction to Scientific and Investigative Techniques*. Boca Raton, Fla.: CRC Press, 2009.

Owen, David. *Police Lab: How Forensic Science Tracks Down and Convicts Criminals*. Toronto: Firefly Books, 2002.

Web Sites

http://www.forensicsciencesimplified.org
The National Forensic Science Technology Center produces this user-friendly Web site that covers the core concepts of all areas of forensic science for nonscientists (or growing ones!).

http://www.crime-scene-investigator.net
This Web site is a trove of information about all the areas of study in the world of crime scene investigation.

http://www.sciencebuddies.org/science-engineering-careers/earth-physical-sciences/forensic-science-technician
Science Buddies is an award-winning Web site devoted to helping students and educators find information about science careers, science fair projects, and family activities.

Series Glossary of Key Terms

airlock a room on a space station from which astronauts can move from inside to outside the station and back

anatomy a branch of knowledge that deals with the structure of organisms

bionic to be assisted by mechanical movements

carbon dioxide a gas that is in the air that we breathe out

classified kept secret from all but a few people in a government or an organization

deforestation the destruction of forest or woodland

diagnose to recognize by signs and symptoms

discipline in science, this means a particular field of study

elite the part or group having the highest quality or importance

genes information stored in cells that determine a person's physical characteristics

geostationary remaining in the same place above the Earth during an orbit

innovative groundbreaking, original

inquisitiveness an ability to be curious, to continue asking questions to learn more

internships jobs often done for free by people in the early stages of study for a career

marine having to do with the ocean

meteorologist a scientist who forecasts weather and weather patterns

physicist a scientist who studies physics, which examines how matter and energy move and relate

primate a type of four-limbed mammal with a developed brain; includes humans, apes, and monkeys

traits a particular quality or personality belonging to a person

Index

Photo Credits

Anti-Doping Agency: 41

Dollar Photo: Doomits 6

Dreamstime: Showface 11, 18, 37 ; Webking 16; Anetlanda 12; Aniram 14; Poutnik 19; Grzegorz Kula 20; CorepicVof 24; Suljo 27; Bogdan Hoda 30; Luchschen 38

Gardner Museum: 34

Newscom: Francine Orr/Kansas City Star 8; Bizu/Splash News 32; Album 35; Sara A. Fajardo/MCT 45

Projectina AG: 28

About the Author

Beth Sutinis is a children's book editor and writer specializing in nonfiction. She lives in Brooklyn, N.Y., with her husband and sons.

Special thanks to Ralph R. Ristenbatt, III, M.S., D-ABC, SCSA-IAI and Christopher J. Hopkins, Director, Forensic Science Graduate Program, University of California, Davis, for their invaluable help and generosity in sharing their wealth of expertise in forensic science and crime scene investigation.